We Read PHONICS™

Track Meet

TREASURE BAY

Parent's Introduction

Welcome to **We Read Phonics**! This series is designed to help you assist your child in reading. Each book includes a story, as well as some simple word games to play with your child. The games focus on the phonics skills and sight words your child will use in reading the story.

Here are some recommendations for using this book with your child:

1 Word Play

There are word games both before and after the story. Make these games fun and playful. If your child becomes bored or frustrated, play a different game or take a break.

Phonics is a method of sounding out words by blending together letter sounds. However, not all words can be "sounded out." **Sight words** are frequently used words that usually cannot be sounded out.

2 Read the Story

After some word play, read the story aloud to your child—or read the story together, by reading aloud at the same time or by taking turns. As you and your child read, move your finger under the words.

Next, have your child read the entire story to you while you follow along with your finger under the words. If there is some difficulty with a word, either help your child to sound it out or wait about five seconds and then say the word.

3 Discuss and Read Again

After reading the story, talk about it with your child. Ask questions like, "What happened in the story?" and "What was the best part?" It will be helpful for your child to read this story to you several times. Another great way for your child to practice is by reading the book to a younger sibling, a pet, or even a stuffed animal!

LEVEL 4

Level 4 introduces words with long "e," "o," and "u" (as in *Pete, nose,* and *flute*) and the long "e" sound made with the vowel pairs "ee" and "ea." It also introduces the soft "c" and "g" sounds (as in *nice* and *cage*), and "or" (as in *sports*).

Track Meet

A We Read Phonics Book: Level 4

Guided Reading: Level D

Reading Consultants: Bruce Johnson, M.Ed., and Dorothy Taguchi, Ph.D.

Published by
Treasure Bay, Inc.
PO Box 519
Roseville, CA 95661 USA

Printed in China

Library of Congress Catalog Card Number: 2024939965

ISBN: 978-1-60115-462-0

Visit us online at:
WeReadPhonics.com

PR-10-24

We Read PHONICS™

Track Meet

By Sindy McKay

Phonics Game

Say the Word

Help your child sound out some of the words from the story.

Materials:
5 simple items (for example, 5 pencils, 5 paper clips, or 5 pennies)

1. Find and point to the word *run* (page 4) in the book. Ask your child to say the separate sounds for each letter. If needed, provide help with the sounds in the word. Then, ask your child to blend the sounds together to say the word. For example, for the word *run*, your child should say the sound for the letter "r," then the sound for the short "u" (as in *up*), then the sound for "n." Your child should then say the word *run*.

2. If your child says the word correctly, give him one item and move on to another simple word that can be sounded out.

3. If your child does not say the word correctly, say the sounds for "r," "u," and "n" yourself, and then blend the sounds together for the word *run*.

4. Continue with additional words from the story that can be sounded out, until your child has all five of the items. Possible words include: *jump, track, meet, teens, fast, race, dash, and place.*

Phonics Game

Word Tic-Tac-Toe

Writing and reading these sight words will help your child read the story.

Materials:

Option 1—Fast and Easy: To print free game materials, go online to WeReadPhonics.com and click **"View & Print: Game Materials."** Then, click on the title for this book.

Option 2—Make Your Own: You'll need: paper or blank cardboard; pencils, crayons, or markers; and a ruler. Optional: If your child has difficulty writing words, write each word on the right on three cards or pieces of paper (one word per card), and play using the cards.

1. Draw on paper a traditional Tic-Tac-Toe board (a 3 x 3 grid).
2. Play this game of Tic-Tac-Toe with a twist. Instead of letters "X" and "O," players choose words from the ones listed below. For example, player 1 chooses the word *like* and player 2 chooses the word *start*. Player 1 says and writes the word like on one of the squares, and player 2 says and writes the word start on one of the squares.
3. The first player to make three in a row, across, up and down, or diagonally, wins the game.
4. Repeat the game with different words from the list below.
from, like, may, over, some, start, your, wish, you

My sister Sage and I like to run!

We like to jump as well!

Track is a sport that lets you run and jump a lot!

On Sunday, I will see my sister run at a track meet.

This track meet is for teens.

The teens will run fast
and jump far!

Some will jump over a hurdle.

Some will use a big pole
to jump over a bar.

In one race, the teens will run far.

The next race will be shorter.

Sage will run in a short race.

She calls her race a dash.

The track meet will be
far from home.

It will be in a huge place.
There will be bleachers to sit on.

When we get there, Sage will greet the girls she will race.

Then all the runners will stretch.

The girls will line up
for the race to start.

On your mark! Get set! Go!
Sage will need a lot of speed
to win!

A judge will keep time for each runner.

She may or may not win,
but Sage will do her best.

I hope to run in a track meet
when I am a teen.

I wish I was at the track meet now!

Phonics Game

I Am Thinking

This is a fun way to practice breaking words into parts, which helps children learn to read new words.

Materials:
5 simple items (for example, 5 pencils, 5 paper clips, or 5 pennies)

1. Explain to your child that the word race has three sounds. Say the three sounds in race: say the sound for "r," long "a" (as in *cake*), and "s." Pause between the three sounds.

2. Ask your child to say all the sounds in the word *meet*. Answer: the sounds for "m," long "e," and "t."

3. When your child is successful, say: "I am thinking of the word *track*. What are the sounds in the word?" Correct answer: "t," "r," "a," and "k."

4. Repeat with the following words. Start with the prompt: "I am thinking of the word . . . . What are the sounds of the word?" Suggested words: *run, jump, fast, pole, dash, greet, judge, speed, win,* and *best*

5. You can extend this activity to two syllable words by asking your child to say the two parts in the word. For the word sister, the answer would be *sis* and *ter*. Suggested two syllable words: *Sunday, over, runner*

Phonics Game

Musical Words

Taking a careful look at the words in the story will help your child to reread those words or patterns another time or in another story.

Materials:

Option 1—Fast and Easy: To print free game materials, go online to WeReadPhonics.com and click **"View & Print: Game Materials."** Then, click on the title for this book.

Option 2—Make Your Own: You'll need 12 index cards and markers or crayons. Write these words on the index cards: **best, dash, greet, judge, meet, place, pole, race, speed, sport, track, win**

1. Place the cards in a circle on the floor facing up and outward. Read the words out loud in random order while your child walks around the outside of the circle.

2. When you stop reading the words, your child stops and picks up the closest word.

3. Your child then reads the word out loud. If he reads it correctly, he keeps the card. If he reads it incorrectly, he puts it back face down.

4. When all of the remaining cards are face down, turn the cards over and repeat. The goal is to correctly read as many cards as possible in round 1.

If you liked ***Track Meet***, here is another **We Read Phonics** book you are sure to enjoy!

Robot Man

After a boy and his dad build a robot man, their life is great! The robot man does all their chores. He even makes them ice cream treats. Their robot does everything for them. But then, robot man falls off the roof and everything goes wrong!